Fashion Accessories

FEATURING RED HEART® BOUTIQUE™ YARNS

The new Red Heart® Boutique™ yarn collection is targeted to the crochet fashionista who loves beautiful textures and colors, but still wants affordable options. The cowl, hat, scarves, and shawls in this book are chic examples of the stylish creations that are possible with the Boutique™ family of yarns. Turn the page to start browsing for your favorite design, and check out the featured yarns beginning on page 47.

About Red Heart® Yarns

Red Heart is one of the most trusted brands in yarn. For over 75 years more people have chosen to make American heirlooms using Red Heart yarn than any other yarn. Red Heart yarns stand for quality, largest color selection, fashion and above all else, crafted with love. Whatever your creativity calls for, you'll find it in the Red Heart family.

LEISURE ARTS, INC.
Maumelle, Arkansas

CRESCENT SHAWL

Designed by Lisa Gentry.

INTERMEDIATE

Finished Size: 48" wide x 16" long (122 cm x 40.5 cm)

SHOPPING LIST

Yarn (Medium Weight) MEDIUM 4

Red Heart® Soft®:

☐ 3729 Grape **A** - 2 balls

Yarn (Super Bulky Weight) SUPER BULKY 6

Red Heart® Boutique Sashay®:

☐ 1960 Boogie **B** - 2 balls

Crochet Hook

☐ 5.5 mm [US I-9]

Additional Supplies

☐ Sewing needle and thread

☐ Yarn needle

GAUGE INFORMATION

(Shell, ch 2) = 1¾" (4.5 cm); 3 Shell rows = 2" (5 cm).

CHECK YOUR GAUGE. Use any size hook to obtain the specified gauge.

– SPECIAL STITCHES –

Shell: (3 Dc, ch 2, 3 dc) in indicated stitch.

V-st: (Dc, ch 1, dc) in indicated stitch.

Ruffle sc: *Skip next mesh loop, go into indicated stitch and pull up a loop with next mesh loop (2 loops on hook), skip next mesh loop, with next mesh loop pull through 2 loops on hook (1 loop remaining—sc made).

SHAWL

With **A**, ch 5; join with a slip st to form a ring.

Row 1 (Wrong side): Ch 4 **(counts as first dc here and throughout)**, 10 dc in ring, do not join — 11 dc.

Row 2 (Right side): Ch 4, turn; 2 dc in each remaining dc across — 21 dc.

Row 3: Ch 4, turn; 2 dc in first dc, [ch 2, skip next 4 dc, shell in next dc] 3 times, ch 2, skip next 4 dc, 3 dc in last dc — 3 shells and 6 dc.

Row 4: [Ch 4, turn; 2 dc in first dc, ch 2, 3 dc in next ch-2 space] **(counts as first shell)**, [ch 2, shell in ch-2 space of next shell] 3 times, ch 2, [3 dc in last ch-2 space, ch 2, 3 dc in last dc] **(counts as last shell)** — 5 shells.

Row 5: Ch 4, turn; 2 dc in first dc, [ch 2, shell in ch-2 space of next shell] 5 times, ch 2, 3 dc in last dc — 5 shells and 6 dc.

Row 6: Ch 4, turn; 2 dc in first dc, [ch 1, dc in next ch-2 space, ch 1, shell in ch-2 space of next shell] 5 times, ch 1, dc in next ch-2 space, ch 1, 3 dc in last dc — 5 shells and 12 dc.

Row 7: Ch 4, turn; 2 dc in first dc, skip next 2 dc, ch 1, V-st in next dc, [ch 1, shell in ch-2 space of next shell, ch 1, V-st in next dc] 5 times, ch 1, 3 dc in last dc — 5 shells, 6 V-sts, and 6 dc.

Row 8: Ch 4, turn; 2 dc in first dc, skip next dc, 3 dc in next dc and in next V-st, [dc in each of next 6 dc, 3 dc in next V-st] 5 times, 3 dc in each of last 2 dc — 60 dc.

Yarn Note: Stretch one end of **B** open for 10" (25.5 cm) and lay flat, with the edge with the metallic thread at the bottom. Work stitches into the top two mesh loop threads of the yarn, leaving the metallic edge loose to form Ruffle.

Row 9 (Wrong side): Ch 1, turn; drop **A** from hook, bring **A** loop and working yarn to front of piece; holding **B** in back of work, pull up a loop in 8th loop of mesh, work ruffle sc in first dc, [skip next dc, ruffle sc in next dc] across, ending with ruffle sc in last dc. Leaving a 4" (10 cm) end, cut **B** — 31 ruffle sc.

Row 10 (Wrong side): With wrong side facing, place **A** loop back on hook; (slip st, ch 4, 3 dc) in first ruffle sc, 2 dc in each of next 29 ruffle sc, 4 dc in last ruffle sc — 66 dc.

Row 11 (Right side): Ch 4, turn; 2 dc in first dc, skip next 2 dc, ch 2, shell in next dc, [ch 2, skip next 5 dc, shell in next dc] 10 times, ch 2, 3 dc in last dc — 11 shells and 6 dc.

Row 12: [Ch 4, turn; 2 dc in first dc, ch 2, skip next dc, 3 dc in next dc] **(counts as first shell)**, ch 2, [shell in ch-2 space of next shell, ch 2] 11 times, [3 dc in next dc, ch 2, 3 dc in last dc] **(counts as last shell)** — 13 shells.

Row 13: Ch 4, turn; 2 dc in first dc, ch 2, shell in ch-2 space of next shell, [ch 1, dc in next ch-2 space, ch 1, shell in ch-2 space of next shell] 12 times, ch 2, 3 dc in last dc — 13 shells and 18 dc.

Row 14: Ch 4, turn; 2 dc in first dc, ch 1, V-st in next ch-2 space, ch 1, shell in ch-2 space of next shell, [ch 1, V-st in next dc, ch 1, shell in ch-2 space of next shell] 12 times, ch 1, V-st in next ch-2 space, ch 1, 3 dc in last dc — 13 shells, 14 V-sts, and 6 dc.

Row 15: Ch 4, turn; 2 dc in first dc, skip next dc, 3 dc in next dc and in next V-st, [dc in each of next 6 dc, 3 dc in next V-St] 13 times, 3 dc in next dc, skip next dc, 3 dc in last dc — 132 dc.

Row 16 (Wrong side): Ch 1, turn; drop **A** from hook, bring **A** loop and working yarn to front of piece; holding **B** in back of work, pull up a loop in 8th loop of mesh, work ruffle sc in first dc, [skip next dc, ruffle sc in next dc] across, ending with ruffle sc in last dc. Leaving a 4" (10 cm) end, cut **B** — 67 ruffle sc.

Row 17 (Wrong side): With wrong side facing, place **A** loop back on hook; (slip st, ch 4, 3 dc) in first ruffle sc, 2 dc in each of next 65 ruffle sc, 4 dc in last ruffle sc — 138 dc.

Row 18 (Right side): Ch 4, turn; 2 dc in first dc, skip next 2 dc, ch 2, shell in next dc, [ch 2, skip next 5 dc, shell in next dc] 22 times, ch 2, 3 dc in last dc — 23 shells and 6 dc.

Row 19: [Ch 4, turn; 2 dc in first dc, ch 2, skip next dc, 3 dc in next dc] **(counts as first shell)**, ch 2, [shell in ch-2 space of next shell, ch 2] 23 times, [3 dc in next dc, ch 2, 3 dc in last dc] **(counts as last shell)** — 25 shells.

Row 20: Ch 4, 2 dc in first dc, ch 2, shell in ch-2 space of next shell, [ch 1, dc in next ch-2 space, ch 1, shell in ch-2 space of next shell] 24 times, ch 2, 3 dc in last dc — 25 shells and 30 dc.

Row 21: Ch 4, turn; 2 dc in first dc, ch 1, V-st in next ch-2 space, ch 1, shell in ch-2 space of next shell, [ch 1, V-st in next dc, ch 1, shell in ch-2 space of next shell] 24 times, ch 1, V-st in next ch-2 space, ch 1, 3 dc in last dc — 25 shells, 26 V-sts, and 6 dc.

Row 22: Ch 4, turn; 2 dc in first dc, skip next dc, 3 dc in next dc and in V-st, [dc in each of next 6 dc, 3 dc in next V-st] 25 times, 3 dc in next dc, skip next dc, 3 dc in last dc — 240 dc.

Row 23 (Wrong side): Ch 1, turn; drop **A** from hook, bring **A** loop and working yarn to front of piece; holding **B** in back of work, pull up a loop in 8th loop of mesh, work ruffle sc in first dc, [skip next dc, ruffle sc in next dc] across, ending with ruffle sc in last dc. Leaving a 4" (10 cm) end, cut **B** — 121 ruffle sc.

Row 24 (Wrong side): With wrong side facing, place **A** loop back on hook; (slip st, ch 4, 3 dc) in first ruffle sc, 2 dc in each of next 119 ruffle sc, 4 dc in last ruffle sc — 246 dc.

Row 25 (Right side): Ch 4, turn; 2 dc in first dc, skip next 2 dc, ch 2, shell in next dc, [ch 2, skip next 5 dc, shell in next dc] 40 times, ch 2, 3 dc in last dc — 41 shells and 6 dc.

Row 26: (Ch 4, turn; 2 dc in first dc, ch 2, skip next dc, 3 dc in next dc] **(counts as first shell)**, ch 2, [shell in ch-2 space of next shell, ch 2] 41 times, [3 dc in next dc, ch 2, 3 dc in last dc] **(counts as last shell)** — 43 shells.

Row 27: Ch 4, turn; 2 dc in first dc, ch 2, [shell in ch-2 space of next shell, ch 2] 43 times, 3 dc in last dc — 43 shells and 6 dc.

Row 28: [Ch 4, turn; 2 dc in first dc, ch 2, skip next dc, 3 dc in next dc] **(counts as first shell)**, [shell in ch-2 space of next shell, ch 2] 43 times, [3 dc in next dc, skip next dc, 3 dc in last dc] **(counts as last shell)** — 45 shells.

Row 29: Ch 1, turn; fasten off **A**, holding **B** in back of work, pull up a loop in 8th loop of mesh, ruffle sc in first 2 dc, *skip next dc, ruffle sc in next ch-2 space, skip next dc, ruffle sc in next dc; repeat from * across, ending with ruffle sc in last dc. Leaving a 4" (10 cm) end, fasten off.

Edging

With right side facing, join **A** with a slip st in end of last row; ch 1, work sc evenly across to center, sc in beginning ring, sc evenly across remaining row ends. Fasten off.

FINISHING

To finish the ends of **B**, fold mesh yarn over the sc edging and tack to WS with sewing needle and thread.

Weave in ends.

MORE BEAUTIFUL CHOICES!

The same Red Heart® Boutique Sashay® that you love now comes in more beautiful choices: Sashay Metallic™ features jeweled shades with all-over metallic for an upscale look; Sashay Sequins™ has replaced the metallic edge with gorgeous sequins.

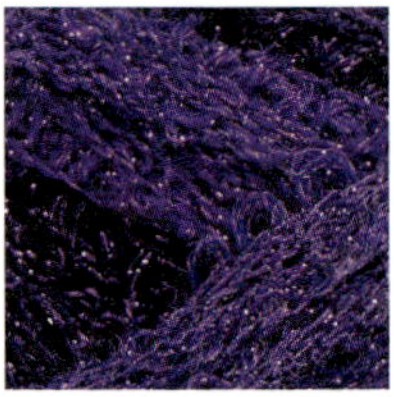

Sashay Metallic™ in 9949 Amethyst

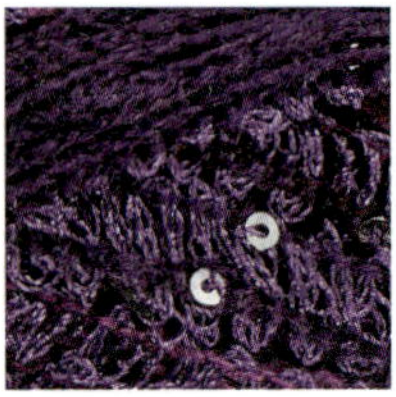

Sashay Sequins™ in 1945 Concord

SWEETHEART RUFFLE SCARF

(Shown on page 11)

Designed by the Red Heart Design Team.

EASY

Scarf measures 52" long (132 cm).

SHOPPING LIST

Yarn (Super Bulky Weight) SUPER BULKY 6

RED HEART® Boutique Sassy Fabric™:

- ☐ 9936 Pink Dot - 1 hank

Crochet Hook

- ☐ 5.5 mm [US I-9]

Additional Supplies

- ☐ Sewing needle and thread

GAUGE INFORMATION

GAUGE is not important for this project.

NOTES

1. Before starting, slide ball band to one end of hank. Remove cardboard from center of hank. Begin your scarf with inside end of Sassy Fabric and continue pulling from inside as you crochet.

2. Note that fabric has holes running along one side ***(see photo below)***. You will be crocheting into each hole.

SCARF

Step 1: Insert hook through 1st hole from back to front; repeat for 2nd, 3rd and 4th holes. You now have 4 holes on the hook.

Step 2: Pinching together all four holes on the hook with left forefinger and thumb, insert hook from front to back into 5th hole and pull through all holes on hook.

Repeat Steps 1 and 2 with each group of 5 holes.

Note: If you put your work down, be sure to put a stitch holder or safety pin on the working stitch. This holder needs to be larger than the hole so that your work will not fall apart.

Continue until scarf is desired length; cut leaving a 3" (7.5 cm) end. Pull end through last stitch and pull tight. Trim beginning and ending fabric strip points so that they blend in with the ruffles. With sewing needle and thread, secure last stitch so scarf will not unravel.

Shake out your scarf so that ruffles spiral.

MITERED SQUARE SHAWL

Designed by Nirmal Kaur Khalsa.

INTERMEDIATE

Shawl measures 15" wide x 50" across longer edge (38 cm x 127 cm).

SHOPPING LIST

Yarn (Medium Weight) MEDIUM 4

RED HEART® Boutique Midnight®:

☐ 1951 Tropical - 8 balls

Crochet Hook

☐ 6mm [J-10 US]

Additional Supplies

☐ Yarn needle

GAUGE INFORMATION

One Square is 5" x 5" (12.75 x 12.75 cm). **CHECK YOUR GAUGE. Use any size hook to obtain the specified gauge.**

– SPECIAL STITCHES –

NOTE: Insert hook in front loop only of sc *(Fig. 2, page 44)*.

sc3togC1 (single crochet corner decrease 1): Insert hook in next st, pull up a loop, skip next st, insert hook in next st, pull up a loop (3 loops on hook), yo and draw through all 3 loops.

Note: "Next st" may be sc or ch.

sc3togC2 (single crochet corner decrease 2): Insert hook in next sc, pull up a loop, insert hook from front to back and to front again around st 1 row below next st, pull up a long loop, skip the st in the current row behind the loop just made, insert hook in next sc of current row, pull up a loop (4 loops on hook), yo and draw through all 4 loops.

NOTES

1. L-shaped shawl is made from 51 square motifs worked in 10 joined sections.
2. Each square is worked off the preceding square beginning with a foundation row. Refer to Assembly Diagram, page 17, for placement.
3. Single crochet is worked in front loops only *(Fig. 2, page 44)*, except where instructed otherwise.
4. Mitered corners are worked over 3 stitches at center of each row.
5. Vary the color patterns by starting some balls from the inside tail and some from the outside.

SHAWL

Square 1

Ch 36.

Note: Single crochet is worked in front loops only *(Fig. 2, page 44)*, except where instructed otherwise.

Row 1 (Wrong side): Working in back bars of ch *(Fig. 1, page 44)*, sc in 2nd ch from hook and in next 15 chs, sc3togC1, sc in remaining 16 chs — 33 sts.

Row 2: Ch 1, turn; sc in first 15 sc, sc3togC2, sc in next 14 sc, working in both loops, sc in last sc — 31 sts.

Row 3: Ch 1, turn; sc in first 14 sc, sc3togC1, sc in next 13 sc, working in both loops, sc in last sc — 29 sts.

Row 4: Ch 1, turn; sc in first 13 sc, sc3togC2, sc in next 12 sc, working in both loops, sc in last sc — 27 sts.

Row 5: Ch 1, turn; sc in first 12 sc, sc3togC1, sc in next 11 sc, working in both loops, sc in last sc — 25 sts.

Row 6: Ch 1, turn; sc in first 11 sc, sc3togC2, sc in next 10 sc, working in both loops, sc in last sc — 23 sts.

Row 7: Ch 1, turn; sc in first 10 sc, sc3togC1, sc in next 9 sc, working in both loops, sc in last sc — 21 sts.

Row 8: Ch 1, turn; sc in first 9 sc, sc3togC2, sc in next 8 sc, working in both loops, sc in last sc — 19 sts.

Row 9: Ch 1, turn; sc in first 8 sc, sc3togC1, sc in next 7 sc, working in both loops, sc in last sc — 17 sts.

Row 10: Ch 1, turn; sc in first 7 sc, sc3togC2, sc in next 6 sc, working in both loops, sc in last sc — 15 sts.

Row 11: Ch 1, turn; sc in first 6 sc, sc3togC1, sc in next 5 sc, working in both loops, sc in last sc — 13 sts.

Row 12: Ch 1, turn; sc in first 5 sc, sc3togC2, sc in next 4 sc, working in both loops, sc in last sc — 11 sts.

Row 13: Ch 1, turn; sc in first 4 sc, sc3togC1, sc in next 3 sc, working in both loops, sc in last sc — 9 sts.

Row 14: Ch 1, turn; sc in first 3 sc, sc3togC2, sc in next 2 sc, working in both loops, sc in last sc — 7 sts.

Row 15: Ch 1, turn; sc in first 2 sc, sc3togC1, sc in next sc, working in both loops, sc in last sc — 5 sts.

Row 16: Ch 1, turn; sc in first sc, sc3togC2, sc in last sc — 3 sts.

Row 17: Turn; working in front loop only, insert hook in first st, pull up a loop, skip next st, working in both loops, insert hook in next st, pull up a loop (3 loops on hook), yo and draw through all 3 loops — 1 st. Do not fasten off.

Squares 2–10

Foundation Row (Right side): Ch 1, turn; sc in last st of Row 17 of previous square, working across ends of rows, work 16 sc evenly spaced across side of previous square — 17 sc.

Row 1: Ch 19, turn; sc in 2nd ch from hook and in next 15 chs, sc3togC1, sc in next 15 sc, working in both loops, sc in last sc — 33 sts.

Rows 2-17: Repeat Rows 2-17 of Square 1.

Fasten off at end of Square 10.

Square 11

Ch 18.

Foundation Row (Right side): With right side facing, insert hook in first square of previous row of squares; working across ends of rows, work 17 sc evenly spaced across first square — 17 sc and 18 chs.

Row 1: Ch 1, turn; sc in first 16 sc, sc3togC1, working in back bars, sc in remaining chs — 33 sts.

Rows 2-17: Repeat Rows 2-17 of Square 1, page 15.

Squares 12–20

Foundation Row (Right side): Ch 1, turn; sc in last st of Row 17 of previous square; working across ends of rows, work 16 sc evenly spaced across side of previous square; working in both loops, sc in last st of square directly below previous square; working across ends of rows, work 17 sc evenly spaced across next square — 35 sc.

Row 1: Ch 1, turn; sc in first 16 sc, sc3togC1, sc in next 15 sc, working in both loops, sc in last sc — 33 sts.

Rows 2-17: Repeat Rows 2-17 of Square 1, page 15.

Fasten off at end of Square 20.

Squares 21–30

Repeat Square 11 once, then repeat Square 12, 9 times.

Fasten off at end of Square 30.

Square 31

Ch 18.

Foundation Row (Right side): With right side facing, insert hook in 8th square of previous row of squares; working across ends of rows, work 17 sc evenly spaced across 8th square — 17 sc and 18 chs.

Row 1: Ch 1, turn; sc in first 16 sc, sc3togC1, working in back bars, sc in remaining chs — 33 sts.

Rows 2-17: Repeat Rows 2-17 of Square 1, page 15.

Squares 32 and 33

Repeat Square 12 twice.

Fasten off at end of Square 33.

Squares 34-36

Repeat Square 11 once, then repeat Square 12 twice.

Fasten off at end of Square 36.

Squares 37-39

Repeat Square 11 once, then repeat Square 12 twice.

Fasten off at end of Square 39.

Assembly Diagram

51	50	49							
48	47	46							
45	44	43							
42	41	40							
39	38	37							
36	35	34							
33	32	31							
30	29	28	27	26	25	24	23	22	21
20	19	18	17	16	15	14	13	12	11
10	9	8	7	6	5	4	3	2	1

Squares 40-42

Repeat Square 11 once, then repeat Square 12 twice.

Fasten off at end of Square 42.

Squares 43-45

Repeat Square 11 once, then repeat Square 12 twice.

Fasten off at end of Square 45.

Squares 46-48

Repeat Square 11 once, then repeat Square 12 twice.

Fasten off at end of Square 48.

Squares 49-51

Repeat Square 11 once, then repeat Square 12 twice.

Fasten off at end of Square 51.

Weave in ends.

BUTTERFLY WRAP

Designed by Double Stitch Twins.

EASY

One size fits most.

SHOPPING LIST

Yarn (Medium Weight)

MEDIUM 4

RED HEART® Boutique Treasure™:

- ☐ 1901 Mosaic **A** - 2 balls
- ☐ 1918 Abstract **B** - 1 ball

Crochet Hook

- ☐ 6.5 mm [US K-10.5]

Additional Supplies

- ☐ Stitch markers
- ☐ Yarn needle

GAUGE INFORMATION

13 dc and 5 rows = 4" (10 cm) using **A. CHECK YOUR GAUGE. Use any size hook to obtain the specified gauge.**

WRAP

With **A**, ch 152.

Row 1: Dc in 4th ch from hook and in next ch, *ch 3, skip next 3 chs, dc in next 3 chs; repeat from * across to last 4 chs, ch 3, skip next 3 chs, dc in last ch — 25 ch-3 spaces.

Row 2: Ch 3 **(counts as dc here and throughout)**, turn; 2 dc in first ch-3 space, *ch 3, skip next 3 dc, 3 dc in next ch-3 space; repeat from * across to last 3 dc, ch 3, skip next 2 dc, dc in last st changing to **B** *(Fig. 4a, page 45)*.

Row 3: With **B**, ch 3, turn; 2 dc in first ch-3 space, *ch 3, skip next 3 dc, 3 dc in next ch-3 space; repeat from * across to last 3 dc, ch 3, skip next 2 dc, dc in last st.

Row 4: Ch 3, turn; 2 dc in first ch-3 space, *ch 3, skip next 3 dc, 3 dc in next ch-3 space; repeat from * across to last 3 dc, ch 3, skip next 2 dc, dc in last st changing to **A**.

Row 5: With **A**, ch 3, turn; 2 dc in first ch-3 space, *ch 3, skip next 3 dc, 3 dc in next ch-3 space; repeat from * across to last 3 dc, ch 3, skip next 2 dc, dc in last st.

Row 6: Ch 2 **(counts as hdc here and throughout)**, turn; 2 hdc in next ch-3 space, *hdc in next 3 dc, 3 hdc in next ch-3 space; repeat from * across to last 3 dc, hdc in last 3 dc changing to **B** in last hdc *(Fig. 4b, page 45)* — 150 hdc.

Row 7: With **B**, ch 1, turn; slip st in first 5 hdc, ch 1, sc in each hdc across to last 5 hdc, leave remaining sts unworked — 140 sc.

Row 8: Ch 3, turn; dc in next sc, *ch 3, skip next sc, dc in next 2 sc; repeat from * across.

Row 9: Ch 3, turn; dc in next dc, *ch 3, dc in next 2 dc; repeat from * across, changing to **A** in last dc.

Rows 10-12: With **A**, ch 3, turn; dc in next dc, *ch 3, dc in next 2 dc; repeat from * across.

Row 13: Ch 2, turn; hdc in next dc, *3 hdc in next ch-3 space, hdc in next 2 dc; repeat from * across, changing to **B** in last hdc.

Row 14: With **B**, ch 1, turn; slip st in first 5 hdc, ch 1, sc in each hdc across to last 5 hdc, leave remaining sts unworked.

Row 15: Ch 3, turn; dc in next sc, skip next sc, *(dc, ch 2, dc) in next sc, skip next sc; repeat from * across to last 2 sc, dc in last 2 sc, changing to **A** in last dc.

Row 16: With **A**, ch 3, turn; dc in next dc, *(dc, ch 2, dc) in next ch-2 space; repeat from * across to last 2 dc, dc in last 2 dc. Place a marker 15" (38 cm) from each side edge.

Row 17: Ch 2, turn; sc in each dc and in each ch-2 space across to first marker, ch 100, sc in each dc and in each ch-2 space across to second marker, ch 100, sc in each dc and in each ch-2 space to end.

Edging Round: Ch 10, turn to work along side edge; sc in edge of Row 13, ch 10, sc in edge of Row 6, ch 10, sc in edge of Row 1, ch 1, turn to work across opposite edge of foundation ch, work 3 sc in each ch-3 space and sc in each dc across, ch 10, turn to work along opposite side edge; sc in edge of Row 6, ch 10, sc in edge of Row 13, ch 10, sc in edge of Row 16, slip st to first st.
Fasten off.

FINISHING

With wrong sides together, fold piece in half along foundation ch, lining up side edges. Measure and mark 9" (23 cm) from side edges along foundation ch. Working through both layers, join **A** with sc in first st ***(see Joining With Sc, page 44)***; sc through both layers to join first and last 9" (23 cm) of foundation ch, continue working through one layer only and sc evenly around unsewn section of foundation ch.
Fasten off.

Weave in ends.

DESIREE'S RUFFLED SCARF

(Shown on pages 24 and 25)

Designed by the Red Heart Design Team.

EASY

Scarf measures 4½" wide x 36" long (11.5 cm x 91.5 cm).

SHOPPING LIST

Yarn (Super Bulky Weight) SUPER BULKY 6

RED HEART® Boutique Sashay Sequins™:

☐ 1505 Fiji **OR**
1938 Cabernet - 1 ball

Crochet Hook

☐ 8 mm [US L-11]

Additional Supplies

☐ Two stitch markers

☐ Sewing needle and thread

GAUGE INFORMATION

5 sts = 4½" (11.5 cm).

Gauge is not important for this project.

Shown in color 1938 Cabernet.

NOTES

1. Stretch one end of the Sashay open for several inches and lay it flat; place the edge with the sequins along the bottom. Notice that the Sashay yarn is a mesh of holes. You will be working with the top of the mesh (railroad track) and leaving the sequin edge loose to form the ruffle.
2. Hook a stitch marker under both top loops of the first sc in each row, moving the markers up each side of the scarf as it progresses.
3. Always turn the work in the same direction at the end of each row.

Note: For a helpful video on crocheting with Sashay, see **www.redheart.com/learn/videos/learn-crochet-boutique-sashay**.

SCARF

Beginning 6" (15 cm) from the raw edge, insert hook through the top of the mesh and pick up a loop. Chain 1, insert and close a stitch marker under both top loops of the ch st, marking the first st. Ch 5 going into every other hole in the mesh.

Row 1: Turn; sc in 2nd ch from hook, marking the sc with a stitch marker. Sc in next 4 chs, removing the stitch marker at the end of the row.

Row 2: Ch 1, turn; sc in each sc across, marking 1st sc in row.

Repeat Row 2 to desired length.

FINISHING

At each end of the scarf, trim the yarn to 6" (15 cm) and tuck the loose end between the nearest two ruffle layers. Using sewing needle and matching thread, tack the end firmly in place.

GRADIENT STRIP SCARF

Designed by Lily M. Chin.

INTERMEDIATE

Scarf measures 7½" wide x 56" long (19 cm x 142 cm), without border.

SHOPPING LIST

Yarn (Medium Weight) MEDIUM 4

Red Heart® Boutique Unforgettable™:

☐ 3945 Parrot - 2 balls

Crochet Hook

☐ 5 mm [US H-8]

Additional Supplies

☐ Yarn needle

GAUGE INFORMATION

9 sc = 2½" (6.25 cm); 17 rows = 4" (10 cm). **CHECK YOUR GAUGE. Use any size hook to obtain the specified gauge.**

— SPECIAL STITCH —

Connector sc: Insert hook in indicated stitch or chain, yo and pull up loop, insert hook into first sc of corresponding row of previously made strip, yo, pull through sc of previously made strip and through both loops on hook.

NOTES

1. Scarf is worked in 3 strips.
2. Strips are joined together using a join-as-you-go technique.
3. In the second and third strips, follow the turning directions carefully so the stitching is worked correctly: in Rows 2 and 4, the slip st must be stitched first, then the fabric is turned, then the single crochets are worked across, and the fabric is turned again at the beginning of the next row. The slip st at the beginning of the row is not only a joining stitch; it replaces the customary "ch 1" before the first single crochet.

SCARF

First Strip

Ch 10.

Row 1 (Right side): Sc in 2nd ch from hook and in each ch across — 9 sc.

Row 2: Ch 1, turn; sc in each sc across.

Repeat Row 2 until piece measures 56" (142 cm) from beginning, end with a wrong side row. Fasten off.

Second Strip

Note: Ensure that right side of previously made strip is facing when joining current strip.

Ch 10.

Row 1 (Right side): Sc in 2nd ch from hook and in next 7 chs, work connector sc in last ch and in first sc of Row 1 on previously made strip — 8 sc and 1 connector sc.

Row 2: With right side facing, slip st in last sc of Row 2 on previously made strip, turn; with wrong side facing, sc in each sc across — 9 sc.

Row 3: Ch 1, turn; sc in first 8 sc, work connector sc in last sc of current row and in first sc of corresponding row on previously made strip — 8 sc and 1 connector sc.

Row 4: With right side facing, slip st in last sc of next row on previously made strip, turn; with wrong side facing, sc in each sc across — 9 sc.

Repeat Rows 3 and 4 until this strip is same length as previously made strip. Fasten off.

Third Strip

Work same as second strip.

Border

Round 1: With right side facing, join yarn with sc in any sc *(see Joining With Sc, page 44)*; sc evenly around, working (sc, ch 2, sc) in each corner; join with a slip st to first sc.

Round 2: Ch 1, turn; *sc in each sc across to next corner ch-2 space, (sc, ch 2, sc) in ch-2 space; repeat from * 3 times, sc in remaining sc across; join with a slip st to first sc.

Round 3: Ch 1, turn; *sc in each sc across to next corner ch-2 space, 3 sc in ch-2 space; repeat from * 3 times, sc in remaining sc across; join with a slip st to first sc. Fasten off.

Weave in ends.

Lightly steam block, if necessary.

SLOUCHY BEANIE

Designed by Ann Regis.

EASY

Hat measures approximately 18" (45.5 cm) circumference at brim.

SHOPPING LIST

Yarn (Medium Weight) MEDIUM 4

Red Heart® Boutique Unforgettable™:

- ☐ 3955 Winery - 1 ball

Crochet Hook

- ☐ 6 mm [US J-10]

Additional Supplies

- ☐ Yarn needle

GAUGE INFORMATION

14 sts and 8 rounds = 4" (10 cm) in pattern.

CHECK YOUR GAUGE. Use any size hook to obtain the specified gauge.

SPECIAL STITCHES

BPdc (back post double crochet): Yo, insert hook from back to front and then to back again around post of next st ***(Fig. 3, page 45)***, yo and pull up loop, [yo and draw through 2 loops on hook] twice.

BPhdc (back post half double crochet): Yo, insert hook from back to front and then to back again around post of next st ***(Fig. 3, page 45)***, yo and pull up loop, yo and draw through all 3 loops on hook.

BPdc2tog (back post double crochet 2 together): [Yo, insert hook from back to front and then to back again around post of next st ***(Fig. 3, page 45)***, yo and pull up a loop, yo and draw through 2 loops on hook] twice, yo and draw through all 3 loops on hook.

hdc2tog (half double crochet 2 together): [Yo, insert hook in next st, yo and pull up loop] twice, yo and draw through all 5 loops on hook.

reverse sc (reverse single crochet): Work sc in opposite direction from which you would usually work ***(Figs. 5a-d, page 46)*** (left to right if you are right-handed and right to left if you are left-handed). This stitch is also known as crab stitch.

NOTES

1. Hat is worked in continuous rounds from top down with right side facing at all times. Do not turn rounds.
2. Repeat Round 3 for all odd-numbered Rounds 5-23; instructions are written for all even-numbered rounds and Round 33.

HAT

Ch 5; join with a slip st to form a ring.

Round 1 (Right side): Ch 3 **(counts as first dc here and throughout)**, 11 dc in ring; join with a slip st to top of beginning ch-3 — 12 dc.

Round 2: Ch 3, dc in same st as joining, 2 dc in each st around; join with a slip st to top of beginning ch-3 — 24 dc.

Round 3 and all odd-numbered rounds through Round 23: Ch 3, work BPdc around each st around; join with a slip st to top of beginning ch-3.

Round 4: Ch 2 **(counts as first hdc here and throughout)**, 2 hdc in next st, *hdc in next st, 2 hdc in next st; repeat from * around; join with a slip st to top of beginning ch-2 — 36 hdc.

Round 6: Ch 2, hdc in next st, 2 hdc in next st, *hdc in next 2 sts, 2 hdc in next st; repeat from * around; join with a slip st to top of beginning ch-2 — 48 hdc.

Round 8: Ch 2, hdc in next 2 sts, 2 hdc in next st, *hdc in next 3 sts, 2 hdc in next st; repeat from * around; join with a slip st to top of beginning ch-2 — 60 hdc.

Round 10: Ch 2, hdc in next 3 sts, 2 hdc in next st, *hdc in next 4 sts, 2 hdc in next st; repeat from * around; join with a slip st to top of beginning ch-2 — 72 hdc.

Round 12: Ch 2, hdc in next 4 sts, 2 hdc in next st, *hdc in next 5 sts, 2 hdc in next st; repeat from * around; join with a slip st to top of beginning ch-2 — 84 hdc.

Round 14: Ch 2, hdc in next 5 sts, 2 hdc in next st, *hdc in next 6 sts, 2 hdc in next st; repeat from * around; join with a slip st to top of beginning ch-2 — 96 hdc.

Round 16: Ch 2, hdc in next 6 sts, 2 hdc in next st, *hdc in next 7 sts, 2 hdc in next st; repeat from * around; join with a slip st to top of beginning ch-2 — 108 hdc.

Rounds 18, 20, and 22: Ch 2, hdc in each st around; join with a slip st to top of beginning ch-2.

Round 24: Ch 2, hdc2tog, *hdc in next st, hdc2tog; repeat from * around; join with a slip st to top of beginning ch-2 — 72 sts.

Rounds 25-27: Ch 3, work BPdc around each st around; join with a slip st to top of beginning ch-3.

Round 28: Ch 3, work BPdc around each of next 6 sts, work BPdc2tog, *work BPdc around each of next 7 sts, work BPdc2tog; repeat from * around; join with a slip st to top of beginning ch-3 — 63 dc.

Rounds 29-32: Ch 3, work BPdc around each st around; join with a slip st to top of beginning ch-3.

Round 33: Ch 2, work BPhdc around each st around; join with a slip st in top of beginning ch-2.

Round 34: Ch 1, work reverse sc in each st around; join with a slip st to first st. Fasten off.

Weave in ends.

CLASSY COWL

(Shown on page 37)

Designed by Lorna Miser.

EASY

Cowl measures 11" wide x 32" circumference (28 cm x 81.5 cm).

SHOPPING LIST

Yarn (Medium Weight) MEDIUM 4

RED HEART® Boutique Swanky™:

☐ 9522 Tealessence - 2 balls

Crochet Hook

☐ 5 mm [US H-8]

Additional Supplies

☐ Yarn needle

☐ Stitch marker

GAUGE INFORMATION

7 V-sts and 10 rows = 4" (10 cm). **CHECK YOUR GAUGE.**

Use any size hook to obtain the specified gauge.

— SPECIAL STITCH —

V-st: (Dc, ch 1, dc) in indicated stitch or space.

NOTE

Cowl is made in joined rounds. Place marker for beginning of round and move marker up as each round is completed.

COWL

Ch 99; taking care not to twist, join with a slip st in first ch. Place marker for beginning of round.

Round 1 (Right side): Ch 4 **(counts as first dc and ch 1 here and throughout)**, dc in same ch as joining (first V-st made), *skip next ch, V-st in next ch; repeat from * around; join with a slip st to 3rd ch of beginning ch-4 — 55 V-sts.

Round 2: Slip st in first ch-1 space, ch 4, dc in same ch-1 space (first V-st made), V-st in each V-st around; join with a slip st to 3rd ch of beginning ch-4.

Repeat Round 2 until piece measures 11" (28 cm). Fasten off.

Weave in ends.

RUFFLED ROSE PIN

Designed by Andee Graves.

EASY

Pin measures about 5" (12.5 cm) diameter.

SHOPPING LIST

Yarn (Medium Weight) MEDIUM 4

RED HEART® Soft®:

☐ 4601 Off White **OR**
5142 Cherry Red **A** - 1 ball

Note: Only about 4 yds (3.75 m) of yarn are needed.

Yarn (Super Bulky Weight) SUPER BULKY 6

RED HEART®
Boutique Sassy Fabric™:

☐ 9936 Pink Dot **OR**
9334 Red Dot **B** - 1 hank

Note: Only about 15 yds (13.75 m) of fabric are needed.

Crochet Hook

☐ 5 mm [US H-8]

Additional Supplies

☐ Stitch marker
☐ 1½" (38 mm) Sew-on pin back
☐ Sewing needle and thread
☐ Yarn needle

GAUGE INFORMATION

3 rounds in pattern measures about 1½" (3.75 cm) across.

CHECK YOUR GAUGE. Use any size hook to obtain the specified gauge.

— SPECIAL STITCH —

RfldSC (ruffled single crochet): With loop of **A** on hook and holding **B** with holes along top, insert hook through a hole from front of fabric to back, [lift hook over top edge of fabric and insert through next hole from front to back] 4 times, insert hook into indicated stitch or space on project, yo and draw loop through project and through fabric on hook until only 2 loops of **A** remain on hook, yo and draw through remaining 2 loops.

SPECIAL TECHNIQUE

Adjustable-slip knot: Create your beginning slip knot as usual but pull up the loop from the beginning tail instead of the working yarn. This allows the first chain loop to be expanded when working the first round of stitches and then closed tightly by pulling on the beginning tail.

NOTES

1. Using an adjustable slip knot at the beginning of the Ruffled Circle makes it easier to work Round 1 and to insert the Sassy Fabric™.
2. All crochet stitches are worked with **A**. **B** is used for embellishment only.

RUFFLED CIRCLE

With **A**, make an adjustable slip knot and place it on hook, ch 2.

Round 1 (Right side): 6 Sc in 2nd ch from hook. Place marker in first sc to indicate beginning of round. Move marker up as each round is completed. Draw about 2½" (6.5 cm) of beginning tail of **B** through open center of round from right side to wrong side. Pull on beginning tail of **A** to close opening tightly around tail of **B**; join with a slip st to first (marked) sc — 6 sc.

Round 2: Ch 1, 2 RfldSC in each of next 6 sts, hold **B** to wrong side of work; join with a slip st to first st — 12 RfldSC.

Fasten off **A**. Cut **B**, leaving a 2½" (6.5 cm) tail.

Shown in color 9334 Red Dot.

PIN BACK CIRCLE

With **A**, leaving an 8" (20.5 cm) beginning tail, make an adjustable slip knot and place it on hook, ch 2.

Round 1 (Right side): 6 Sc in 2nd ch from hook; join with a slip st to first sc — 6 sc.

Round 2: Ch 1, 2 sc in each st around; join with a slip st to first sc — 12 sc.

Round 3: Ch 1, [sc in next st, 2 sc in next st] 6 times; join with a slip st to first sc — 18 sc.
Fasten off, leaving a 10" (25.5 cm) tail.

FINISHING

Finish Ruffled Circle: Weave in tails of **A**. On wrong side, tie ends of **B** together tightly with a square knot. Trim excess fabric.

Finish Pin Back Circle: With beginning tail, sew pin back to right side of pin back circle. Weave in remainder of beginning tail on wrong side.

Assemble: Hold ruffled circle and pin back circle with wrong sides together and pin back circle centered on ruffled circle. With ending tail sew pin back circle to ruffled circle sewing through tops of Round 2 sts of ruffled circle and into gully between Rounds 2 and 3 of pin back circle.

Weave in any remaining ends.

GENERAL INSTRUCTIONS

ABBREVIATIONS

A, B, etc.	color A, B, etc.
BPdc	Back Post double crochet(s)
BPdc2tog	Back Post double crochet 2 together
BPhdc	Back Post half double crochet(s)
ch(s)	chain(s)
cm	centimeters
dc	double crochet(s)
hdc	half double crochet(s)
hdc2tog	half double crochet 2 together
mm	millimeters
RfldSC	Ruffled Single Crochet
sc	single crochet(s)
sc3tog	single crochet 3 together
st(s)	stitch(es)
yo	yarn over

SYMBOLS & TERMS

( ) **or** [ ] = work directions in parentheses or brackets the number of times specified.

* = repeat whatever follows the * as indicated.

CROCHET HOOKS	
U.S.	**Metric mm**
B-1	2.25
C-2	2.75
D-3	3.25
E-4	3.5
F-5	3.75
G-6	4
7	4.5
H-8	5
I-9	5.5
J-10	6
K-10½	6.5
L-11	8
M/N-13	9
N/P-15	10
P/Q	15
Q	16
S	19

CROCHET TERMINOLOGY		
UNITED STATES		INTERNATIONAL
slip stitch (slip st)	=	single crochet (sc)
single crochet (sc)	=	double crochet (dc)
half double crochet (hdc)	=	half treble crochet (htr)
double crochet (dc)	=	treble crochet (tr)
treble crochet (tr)	=	double treble crochet (dtr)
double treble crochet (dtr)	=	triple treble crochet (ttr)
triple treble crochet (tr tr)	=	quadruple treble crochet (qtr)
skip	=	miss

BEGINNER	Projects for first-time crocheters using basic stitches. Minimal shaping.
EASY	Projects using yarn with basic stitches, repetitive stitch patterns, simple color changes, and simple shaping and finishing.
INTERMEDIATE	Projects using a variety of techniques, such as basic lace patterns or color patterns, mid-level shaping and finishing.
EXPERIENCED	Projects with intricate stitch patterns, techniques and dimension, such as non-repeating patterns, multi-color techniques, fine threads, small hooks, detailed shaping and refined finishing.

Yarn Weight Symbol & Names	LACE 0	SUPER FINE 1	FINE 2	LIGHT 3	MEDIUM 4	BULKY 5	SUPER BULKY 6
Type of Yarns in Category	Fingering, 10-count crochet thread	Sock, Fingering Baby	Sport, Baby	DK, Light Worsted	Worsted, Afghan, Aran	Chunky, Craft, Rug	Bulky, Roving
Crochet Gauge* Ranges in Single Crochet to 4" (10 cm)	32-42 double crochets**	21-32 sts	16-20 sts	12-17 sts	11-14 sts	8-11 sts	5-9 sts
Advised Hook Size Range	Steel*** 6,7,8 Regular hook B-1	B-1 to E-4	E-4 to 7	7 to I-9	I-9 to K-10½	K-10½ to M/N-13	M/N-13 and larger

*GUIDELINES ONLY: The chart above reflects the most commonly used gauges and hook sizes for specific yarn categories.

** Lace weight yarns are usually crocheted on larger-size hooks to create lacy openwork patterns. Accordingly, a gauge range is difficult to determine. Always follow the gauge stated in your pattern.

*** Steel crochet hooks are sized differently from regular hooks–the higher the number the smaller the hook, which is the reverse of regular hook sizing.

GAUGE

Gauge refers to the number of stitches and rows in a given area. When making projects, ensure that your project is the correct finished size and is to gauge. Work the area as stated in the pattern and then measure to check that it agrees with the gauge given. If it is not the same size, change your hook size. If it is too large, use a smaller hook. If it is too small, use a larger hook size.

JOINING WITH SC

When instructed to join with sc, begin with a slip knot on hook. Insert hook in stitch or space indicated, yo and pull up a loop, yo and draw through both loops on hook.

BACK BAR

Work only in loops indicated by arrows *(Fig. 1)*.

Fig. 1

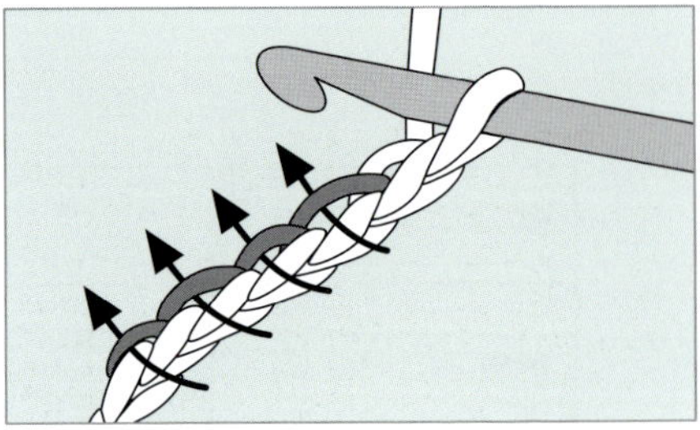

FRONT LOOPS ONLY

Work only in loop(s) indicated by arrow *(Fig. 2)*.

Fig. 2

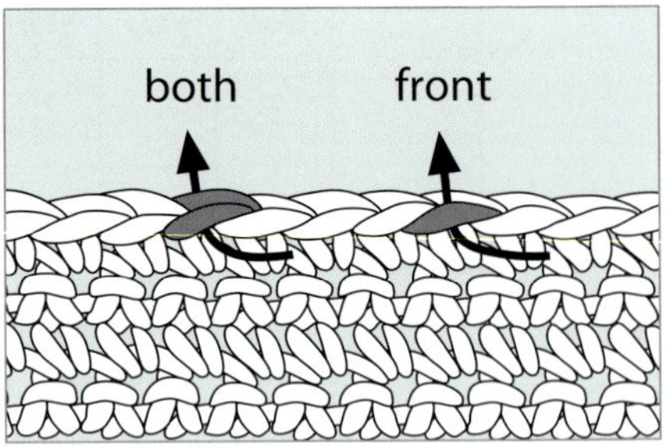

POST STITCH

Work around the post of the stitch indicated, inserting the hook in direction of the arrow *(Fig. 3)*.

Fig. 3

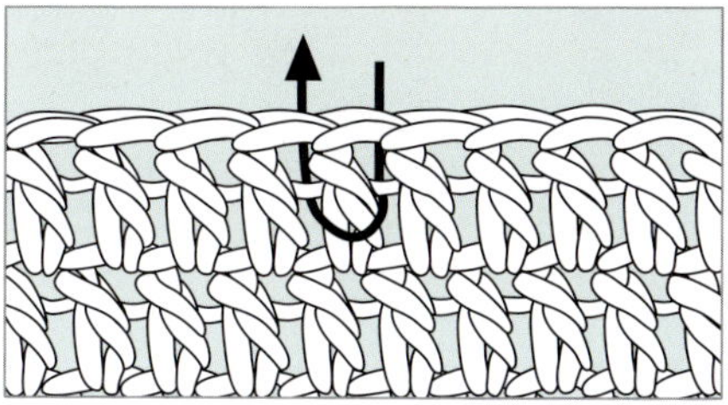

CHANGING COLORS

Work the last stitch to within one step of completion, hook new yarn *(Fig. 4a or 4b)* and draw through all loops on hook. Cut old yarn and work over both ends.

Fig. 4a

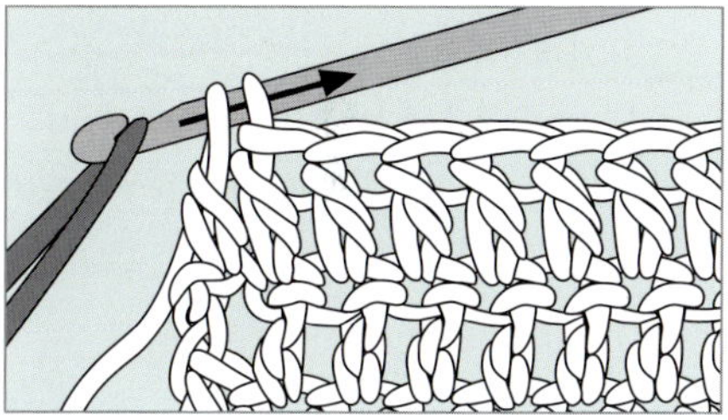

Fig. 4b

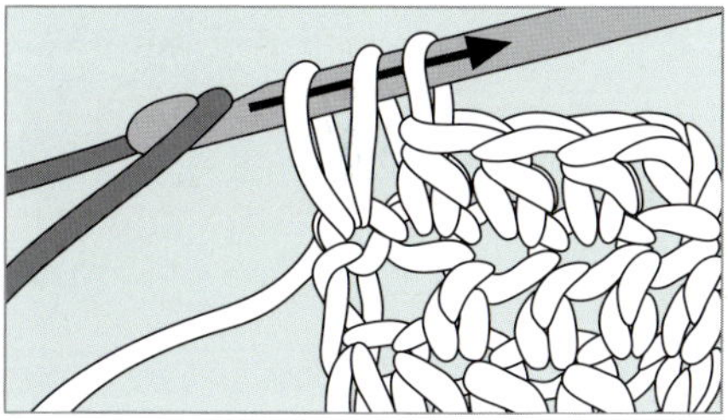

REVERSE SINGLE CROCHET

Working from **left** to **right**, *insert hook in st to right of hook *(Fig. 5a)*, yo and draw through, under and to the left of loop on hook (2 loops on hook) *(Fig. 5b)*, yo and draw through both loops on hook *(Fig. 5c)* **(reverse sc made, *Fig. 5d*)**; repeat from * around.

Fig. 5a

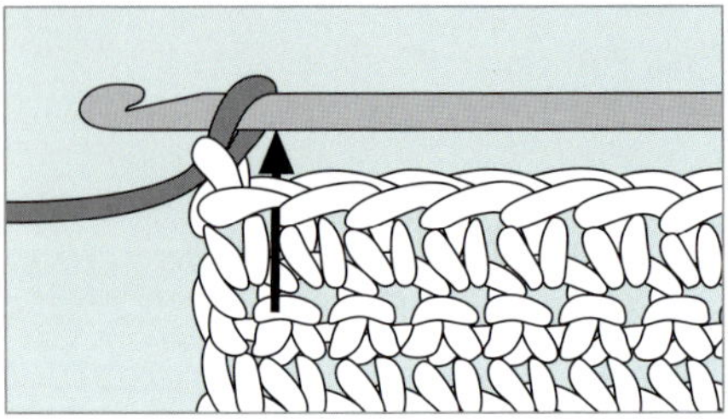

Fig. 5b

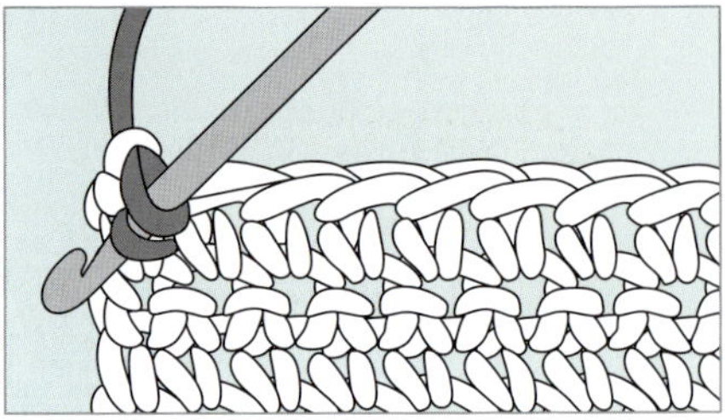

Fig. 5c

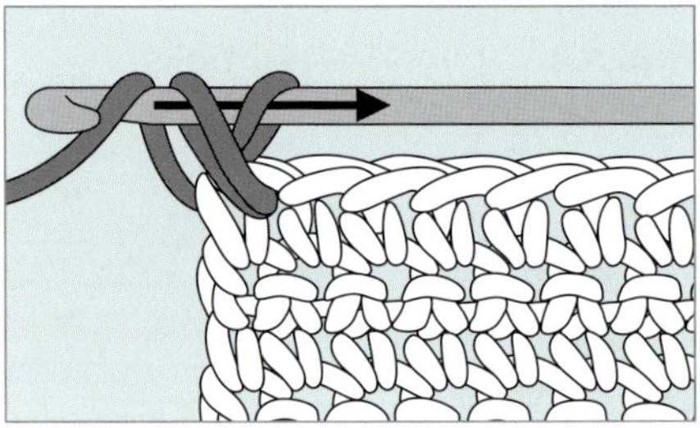

Fig. 5d

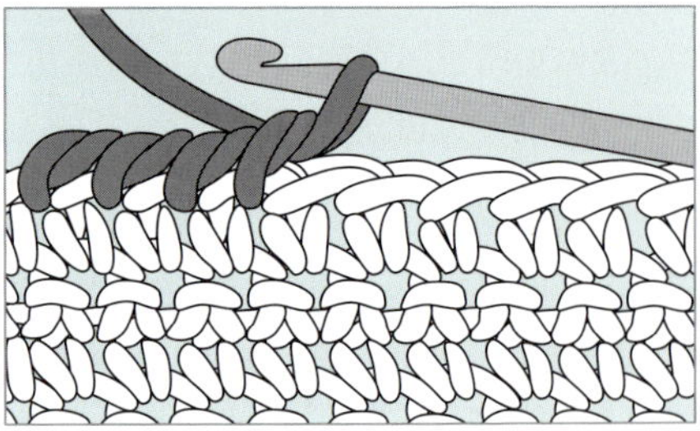

YARN INFORMATION

The projects in this book were created with **RED HEART®** yarns. For best results, we recommend following the pattern exactly as written. Be sure to purchase the amounts recommended in the pattern, and retain your labels. Always follow the care instructions provided on the label.

RED HEART® Soft® MEDIUM 4
Art. E728 available in solid colors 5 oz (141 g), 256 yd (234 m), prints 4 oz (113 g), 204 yds (187 m), heather 4 oz (113 g), 212 yd (194 m) balls.

RED HEART® MEDIUM 4
Boutique Treasure™
Art. E788 available in 3.5 oz. (100 g), 151 yd (138 m) balls

RED HEART® MEDIUM 4
Boutique Swanky™
Art. E819 available in 3.5 oz. (100 g), 202 yd (185 m) balls

RED HEART® MEDIUM 4
Boutique Unforgettable™
Art. E793 available in 3.5 oz (100 g), 280 yd (256 m) balls

RED HEART® SUPER BULKY 6
Boutique Sashay™
Art. E782, available in 3.5 oz (100 g), 30 yd (27 m) balls

RED HEART® SUPER BULKY 6
Boutique Sashay Sequins™
Art. E782S, available in 3.5 oz (100 g), 20 yd (18 m) balls

RED HEART® SUPER BULKY 6
Boutique Midnight®
Art. E786, available in 2.5 oz (70 g), 153 yd (140 m) balls

RED HEART® SUPER BULKY 6
Boutique Sassy Fabric™
Art. E818 available in prints 30 yd (27 m) hanks

For more ideas and inspiration

- www.redheart.com
- www.facebook.com/redheartyarns
- www.pinterest.com/redheartyarns
- www.twitter.com/redheartyarns
- www.youtube.com/redheartyarns
- Instagram@redheartyarns